STRENGTHENED TO SERVE

2 CORINTHIANS

12 Studies for Individuals or Groups

JIM & CAROL PLUEDDEMANN

SHAW

We dedicate this book to our mothers,
Mary Margaret Plueddemann and Wilda Savage,
who have shown us what it means to serve
and who have taught us to live
more by faith and less by sight (2 Corinthians 5:7).

STRENGTHENED TO SERVE
A SHAW BOOK
PUBLISHED BY WATERBROOK PRESS
5446 North Academy Boulevard, Suite 200
Colorado Springs, CO 80918
A division of Random House, Inc.

Unless otherwise indicated, all Scripture quotations are taken from the *Holy Bible: New International Version* ® *NIV* ® Copyright © 1973, 1978, 1984 by International Bible Society. Used by permission of Zondervan Publishing House. All rights reserved.

"That the glory may be of God" on page 5 is reprinted from *The Sighting,* © 1981 by Luci Shaw and is used by permission of Harold Shaw Publishers.

ISBN: 9780877887836

Printed in the United States of America

146502721

CONTENTS

That the glory may be of God

Each day he seems to shine
from the more primitive pots
the battered bowls.

Service may polish silver &
gold up to honor
& I could cry to glitter
like porcelain
or lead crystal

But light is a clearer
contrast through my cracks
& flame is cleaner seen
if its container
does not compete

Luci Shaw

INTRODUCTION

God has called each of us to serve. But what does "successful ministry" look like? Second Corinthians is an intensely personal, autobiographical letter in which Paul opens his mind and heart to people he loves very much. In it we see Paul's passion and his way of dealing with the problems of the early church. We see his love for the church, the pain he felt over misunderstanding, and the cost of his sufferings. But there is also a great deal we don't see. Reading Paul's letter is something like listening to one side of a telephone conversation. We don't have the letter that he was answering and we don't know fully the circumstances that prompted him to write his letter.

Corinth was a rich commercial seaport in Greece with a population of about a half million. It was noted for its sexual license and had a reputation for moral corruption. A luxury-loving city, it had a ratio of two slaves to every free person.

Paul visited Corinth on his second missionary journey around A.D. 50 (Acts 18:1-18). He founded the church there and stayed a year and a half on that first visit. Apollos, a gifted preacher from Alexandria, later strengthened and extended the young church (Acts 18:24–19:1). Paul indirectly refers to a second "painful visit" in 2 Corinthians 2:1. This visit apparently resulted in severe conflict with false apostles who attacked Paul's credibility as a true apostle.

Before writing 2 Corinthians, Paul had already written three letters to the Corinthians. Two of these are now lost (one referred to in 1 Corinthians 5:9 and the "painful" letter referred to in 2 Corinthians

2:3). Some scholars think that parts of them may be preserved in 2 Corinthians 6:14–7:1 and chapters 10–13.

This letter was written to prepare the Corinthians for Paul's third and last visit to Corinth (Acts 19:21; 20:1-3) in A.D. 57 or 58.

The false teachers at Corinth taught that Christians ought to be free from suffering. Paul, on the other hand, taught that suffering should be expected, especially by Christians. Against the false triumphalism of his opponents, Paul showed that God's power is demonstrated best in human weakness. Like Paul, we too can be confident in weakness, strengthened by struggle to serve a hurting world.

HOW TO USE THIS STUDYGUIDE

Fisherman studyguides are based on the inductive approach to Bible study. Inductive study is discovery study; we discover what the Bible says as we ask questions about its content and search for answers. This is quite different from the process in which a teacher *tells* a group *about* the Bible and what it means and what to do about it. In inductive study God speaks directly to each of us through his Word.

A group functions best when a leader keeps the discussion on target, but this leader is neither the teacher nor the "answer person." A leader's responsibility is to *ask*—not *tell*. The answers come from the text itself as group members examine, discuss, and think together about the passage.

There are four kinds of questions in each study. The first is an *approach question*. Used before the Bible passage is read, this question breaks the ice and helps you focus on the topic of the Bible study. It begins to reveal where thoughts and feelings need to be transformed by Scripture.

Some of the earlier questions in each study are *observation questions* designed to help you find out basic facts—who, what, where, when, and how.

When you know what the Bible says you need to ask, *What does it mean?* These *interpretation questions* help you to discover the writer's basic message.

Application questions ask, *What does it mean to me?* They challenge you to live out the Scripture's life-transforming message.

Fisherman studyguides provide spaces between questions for jotting down responses and related questions you would like to raise in the group. Each group member should have a copy of the studyguide and may take a turn in leading the group.

A group should use any accurate, modern translation of the Bible such as the *New International Version*, the *New American Standard Bible*, the *Revised Standard Version*, the *New Jerusalem Bible*, or the *Good News Bible*. (Other translations or paraphrases of the Bible may be referred to when additional help is needed.) Bible commentaries should not be brought to a Bible study because they tend to dampen discussion and keep people from thinking for themselves.

SUGGESTIONS FOR GROUP LEADERS

1. Read and study the Bible passage thoroughly beforehand, grasping its themes and applying its teachings for yourself. Pray that the Holy Spirit will "guide you into truth" so that your leadership will guide others.

2. If the studyguide's questions ever seem ambiguous or unnatural to you, rephrase them, feeling free to add others that seem necessary to bring out the meaning of a verse.

3. Begin (and end) the study promptly. Start by asking someone to pray for God's help. Remember, the Holy Spirit is the teacher, not you!

4. Ask for volunteers to read the passages out loud.

5. As you ask the studyguide's questions in sequence, encourage everyone to participate in the discussion. If some are silent, ask, "What do you think, Heather?" or, "Dan, what can you add to that answer?" or suggest, "Let's have an answer from someone who hasn't spoken up yet."

6. If a question comes up that you can't answer, don't be afraid to admit that you're baffled! Assign the topic as a research project for someone to report on next week.

7. Keep the discussion moving and focused. Though tangents will inevitably be introduced, you can bring the discussion back to the topic at hand. Learn to pace the discussion so that you finish a study each session you meet.

8. Don't be afraid of silences: some questions take time to answer and some people need time to gather courage to speak. If silence persists, rephrase your question, but resist the temptation to answer it yourself.

9. If someone comes up with an answer that is clearly illogical or unbiblical, ask him or her for further clarification: "What verse suggests that to you?"

10. Discourage Bible-hopping and overuse of cross-references. Learn all you can from *this* passage, along with a few important references suggested in the studyguide.

11. Some questions are marked with a ♦. This indicates that further information is available in the Leader's Notes at the back of the guide.

12. For further information on getting a new Bible study group started and keeping it functioning effectively, read Gladys Hunt's *You Can Start a Bible Study Group* and *Pilgrims in Progress: Growing through Groups* by Jim and Carol Plueddemann.

SUGGESTIONS FOR GROUP MEMBERS

1. Learn and apply the following ground rules for effective Bible study. (If new members join the group later, review these guidelines with the whole group.)

2. Remember that your goal is to learn all that you can *from the Bible passage being studied.* Let it speak for itself without using Bible commentaries or other Bible passages. There is more than enough in each assigned passage to keep your group productively occupied for one session. Sticking to the passage saves the group from insecurity and confusion.

3. Avoid the temptation to bring up those fascinating tangents that don't really grow out of the passage you are discussing. If the topic is of common interest, you can bring it up later in informal conversation following the study. Meanwhile, help each other stick to the subject!

4. Encourage each other to participate. People remember best what they discover and verbalize for themselves. Some people are naturally shyer than others, or they may be afraid of making a mistake. If your discussion is free and friendly and you show real interest in what other group members think and feel, they will be more likely to speak up. Remember, the more people involved in a discussion, the richer it will be.

5. Guard yourself from answering too many questions or talking too much. Give others a chance to express themselves. If you are one who participates easily, discipline yourself by counting to ten before you open your mouth!

6. Make personal, honest applications and commit yourself to letting God's Word change you.

COMFORTED TO COMFORT

2 Corinthians 1:1-11

One of the most difficult kinds of letters to write is a "sympathy note." Have you noticed that the most comforting notes are often written by those who have had firsthand experience with sorrow themselves?

In this letter, Paul writes to suffering people from the perspective of one who has also suffered. In fact, Paul sees a direct correlation between his suffering and the comfort he offers.

◆ **1.** Describe a time when you were comforted by someone or a time when you were a means of comfort to another person.

Read 2 Corinthians 1:1-11.

♦ **2.** What authority does Paul claim as he writes this letter?

3. In what ways are "grace and peace" (verse 2) a summary of the Good News and of ultimate comfort?

.

4. How does Paul's description of God (verse 3) help you to understand God's nature?

5. What principles about suffering and comfort can you learn from verses 4-7? What practical examples of these principles have you experienced?

♦ **6.** How does Paul's description of his suffering make you feel (verses 8-11)?

7. What had Paul learned about himself through his suffering? About God?

8. What confidence does Paul affirm (verse 10)?

9. What help does Paul need from the Corinthians? What will be the result of this help?

10. Can you think of a time when God helped you not only to endure suffering but also to experience benefits from it?

♦ **11.** Where are you right now in terms of comfort—are you experiencing comfort, giving comfort, or in need of comfort? What does this passage suggest for your needs?

♦ **12.** Pray together, asking God to help you set your hope on him (verse 10) and to make your life a comfort to someone who is suffering. Identify individuals within your group or outside of it who need your prayers for comfort or deliverance (verses 10-11).

TOUGH LOVE

2 Corinthians 1:12–2:11

Second Corinthians is a letter about relationships—not perfect ones, but real ones. We experience our greatest joys and our deepest griefs in relationships with those we care about the most.

Paul was struggling in his relationships with the believers in Corinth and he doesn't try to hide this conflict at all. Instead he pours out his soul, dealing head-on with issues of trust, motives, rebuke, and reconciliation. As we look into his heart, we see the heart of the Christian message—the good news that Christ meets our deepest relational needs.

1. Tell of a time when you were disappointed or disillusioned because of a change of plans.

Read 2 Corinthians 1:12–2:4.

♦ **2.** From the clues in these verses, of what may Paul have been accused?

3. What characterized Paul's and Timothy's conduct (verses 12-14)?

♦ **4.** What does Paul affirm about God's promises?

♦ **5.** What has God done to help us stand firm in Christ (verses 21-22)? What is our part in standing firm (verse 24)?

6. Why did Paul change his plans?

♦ **7.** What do you learn about Paul as a person and as a leader in this passage?

Read 2 Corinthians 2:5-11.

♦ **8.** What seems to have been the response to Paul's painful letter?

♦ **9.** What principles of punishment and forgiveness does Paul teach?

10. Is there someone you or your church fellowship needs to forgive and comfort? Take a moment to pray silently for that person and your response to him or her.

11. What encouragement can you take from this passage? What challenge?

LIVING LETTERS

2 Corinthians 2:12–3:6

Whether we like it or not, people judge Christ by his followers. Every Christian is an advertisement for Christianity. Paul speaks in this passage about the fragrance Christians spread. He also describes Christians as open letters that all can read. This is an awesome responsibility from which we might be tempted to shrink. Even Paul cries, "Who is equal to such a task?" This passage answers his question.

1. God gives every Christian tasks of service. Describe a time when you felt incompetent to do a particular task. Or describe a time when you felt God gave you special competence. What factors contributed to your confidence or lack of confidence?

Read 2 Corinthians 2:12–3:6.

♦ **2.** Paul didn't know if he should stay in Troas or leave. What factors influenced Paul's decision? What can we learn from this about how God can lead us?

3. In what sense can we be thankful and triumphant even in the midst of personal struggles (verse 14)?

4. How does the metaphor of Christianity spreading like a fragrance challenge you?

♦ **5.** Why does this aroma have contrasting effects?

6. Some Christian leaders today are accused of having selfish motives for their ministry. Describe some current examples of people who "peddle the word of God for profit" (verse 17). What examples have you seen of those who "speak before God with sincerity, like men sent from God" (verse 17)? Describe someone who has been either a negative or positive role model for you in ministry.

7. What results do people typically look for in a "successful ministry"? Contrast this typical view of success with the results to which Paul pointed (verse 3).

8. False teachers in the church were claiming that Paul wasn't a real apostle. What evidence did Paul cite as his personal letter of recommendation?

9. What would your letter of recommendation look like for your ministry?

♦ **10.** What is the source of Paul's confidence and competence (verses 4-6)? How does this contrast with the popular definition of competence? What implications does this have in terms of who can minister?

11. As we serve in ministry, we tend to become either self-sufficient and proud or paralyzed by a feeling of inferiority. Into which trap do you tend to fall? How can verses 4-6 keep us from either pitfall?

12. Look again at the whole passage. What are the most important principles of ministry for you personally? How does Paul's teaching encourage you in your ministry? Why are these principles important for the church today?

UNFADING GLORY

2 Corinthians 3:7–4:18

A story is told of an ugly man who fell in love with a beautiful woman. In order to impress the woman, he put on a mask of a handsome person. As the story goes, he left the mask on so long that his face was molded to the shape of the mask.

Today's passage talks about being transformed into Christ's likeness. In Paul's life, that process included suffering. He even talks about being given over to death for Jesus' sake. But the dominant theme of these verses is glory—an eternal glory that far outweighs momentary troubles.

1. What is the most glorious thing you have experienced— a sunset? A work of art or a musical performance? How long did it last?

Read 2 Corinthians 3:7-18.

♦ **2.** How does Paul contrast the new covenant to the old covenant? (Look also at verse 6 from last week's passage.)

3. Have you had moments of personal glory when people thought you were wonderful? How long did the experience last? Compare this with the two kinds of glory described in verses 7-18.

♦ **4.** What are the practical results of the new covenant or new ministry that Paul describes (verses 12-18)?

5. How have you seen the glory of Christ reflected in another person? What did this look like?

Read 2 Corinthians 4:1-18.

◆ **6.** What is the treasure Paul speaks of in verse 7?

◆ **7.** What can we learn about presenting the gospel in this passage? About the content of the gospel?

8. What truth does Paul illustrate by the paradox of treasure stored in clay (verse 7)?

9. Explore the other paradoxes in this passage. In what ways do these contrasts describe your own life?

10. What is the basis for Paul's double affirmation that "we do not lose heart" (verses 1 and 16)?

11. Sometimes Christians are accused of being "so heavenly minded that they are of no earthly use." How do these verses contradict that idea?

12. What was Paul willing to die for? What are you willing to die for?

13. What are you doing with the treasure God has entrusted to you?

AT HOME WITH THE LORD

2 Corinthians 5:1-10

"Where's your home?" Many of us cringe at that question, not really sure how to answer. In our transitory society, we find ourselves longing for permanence and a sense of rootedness. Our driver's license shows our official address, but often that address doesn't match our real sense of where home is.

Paul experienced that tension too. His body was on earth, but his heart was in heaven. He recognized that his body was a very temporary structure and longed for the eternal shelter that awaited him in heaven. But meanwhile, with one foot in time and one in eternity, he devoted himself to the goal of pleasing God—and challenges us to do the same.

1. Where is "home" for you?

Read 2 Corinthians 5:1-10.

◆ **2.** Why is a tent a good picture of our earthly body?

3. In what ways do we feel "naked" here in this world?

◆ **4.** How does Paul describe the "heavenly dwelling"?

5. What makes Paul so confident about his future (verse 5)?

♦ **6.** How does Paul's confidence affect his view of life and death?

7. Why do you think we often live as if we prefer to be "at home in the body"?

8. What was Paul's consuming life goal?

9. Think about the week ahead. Considering your priorities and plans, whom are you living to please?

♦ **10.** How much does fear of judgment motivate you (verse 10)? How much do you think it motivated Paul?

11. What will it mean for you to "live by faith, not by sight" this week? In the next five years?

AMBASSADORS FOR CHRIST

2 Corinthians 5:11–6:13

To be selected as an ambassador to another country is a great honor. It also carries enormous responsibility. Today's passage declares that we are ambassadors for Christ. What are the implications of this assignment? Paul's picture is not one of glamour, but of hardship, trouble, and sleepless nights. But the rewards are there, too— "having nothing, and yet possessing everything" (6:10). What could motivate someone for this task? You'll discover the answer in today's study.

♦ **1.** Who was Christ's ambassador to you? How did you hear about the message of reconciliation?

Read 2 Corinthians 5:11-15.

♦ **2.** What were Paul's motives for ministry? How do these
motives fit together?

Read 2 Corinthians 5:16–6:2.

3. What might it mean to regard someone from a worldly
point of view?

4. What does "reconciliation" mean? (Look up the word
in a dictionary.) Describe a time when you were alienated
from someone and then reconciled.

♦ **5.** How does this passage describe the reconciliation God has provided for us?

6. What is our responsibility as Christ's ambassadors?

Read 2 Corinthians 6:3-13.

7. How does Paul model the responsibility of an ambassador toward the Corinthians?

♦ **8.** What resources for ministry do you see in this passage?

9. What kind of "results" does Paul have to boast about at this point in his ministry with the Corinthians?

10. How do Paul's results compare or contrast to the "marks of success" we look for in ministry today?

11. How does Paul's example challenge or encourage you in terms of your own ministry?

12. Who needs your ministry of reconciliation this week?

PURITY AND PROMISE

2 Corinthians 6:14–7:16

Our last study ended with Paul's plea—"open wide your hearts" (6:13). In today's passage, Paul seems to be saying, "Open wide your hearts—but not to everyone." What does it mean to be pure and separate? And how does the challenge of purity relate to our responsibility to be Christ's ambassadors?

1. Describe a time when you have experienced the tension of wanting to be separate and pure, yet also wanting to relate to unbelievers.

Read 2 Corinthians 6:14–7:1.

♦ **2.** The command in 6:14 is often applied to marriages between believers and unbelievers. What other relationships
might it include?

3. What contrasts between believers and unbelievers does
Paul use to support his command?

4. What promises does Paul refer to in 7:1? How do these
promises provide motivation for being pure?

---

5. How does it make you feel to know you are the dwelling place of the living God (verse 16)? What difference should this make in the relationships you form?

♦ **6.** How can you "be separate" (verse 17) and also be an ambassador for Christ (5:20)?

Read 2 Corinthians 7:2-16.

7. What plea does Paul repeat in verse 2? What reasons does he give to support his request?

8. What reasons does Paul have to be confident, proud, and joyful (verse 4) about the Corinthians? (Look at the whole passage.)

♦ **9.** What were the effects of the "godly sorrow" the Corinthians experienced? What might characterize "worldly sorrow"?

10. Why is sorrow for sin healthy and appropriate? What examples have you seen of godly grief?

11. If there is a need in your life for godly sorrow, confess it to God now in silent prayer.